The 30 Hour Day

*Develop Achiever's Mindset and Habits,
Work Smarter and Still Create Time For
Things That Matter*

SOM BATHLA

Your Free Gift Bundle

As a token of my thanks for taking out time to read my book, I would like to offer you a gift pack:

Click and Download your Free Gift Bundle Below

You can also grab your FREE GIFT BUNDLE through this below URL:

http://sombathla.com/freegiftbundle

More Books by Som Bathla

WHAT IF I FAIL?: Leverage your Fear of Failure & Turn into Fuel for Success, Rewire your Belief System, Learn to Trigger Action despite being Scared and Take Charge of Your Life

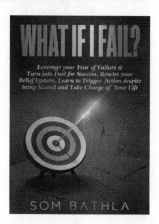

THE MINDSET MAKEOVER: Transform Your Mindset to Attract Success, Unleash Your True Potential, Control Thoughts and Emotions, Become Unstoppable and Achieve Your Goals Faster

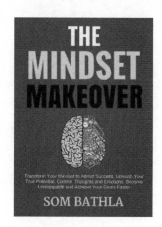

3

Living Beyond Self Doubt: Reprogram Your Insecure Mindset, Reduce Stress and Anxiety, Boost Your Confidence, Take Massive Action despite Being Scared & Reclaim Your Dream Life

FOCUS MASTERY: Master Your Attention, Ignore Distractions, Make Better Decisions Faster and Accelerate Your Success

JUST GET IT DONE: Conquer Procrastination, Eliminate Distractions, Boost Your Focus, Take Massive Action Proactively and Get Difficult Things Done Faster

Master Your Day- Design Your Life: Develop Growth Mindset, Build Routines to Level-Up your Day, Deal Smartly with Outside World and Craft Your Dream Life

The Quoted Life: 223 Best Inspirational and Motivational Quotes on Success, Mindset, Confidence, Learning, Persistence, Motivation, and Happiness

For More details and subscribing to the newsletter, please visit www.sombathla.com

CONTENTS

INTRODUCTION

WHY YOU SHOULD READ THIS BOOK

"If you are not willing to learn, no one can help you. But if you are determined to learn no one can stop you."

Great, now you have this book in your hands and started reading. So firstly let's discuss why you should read this book at all.

Yes, the title attracts you with a promise for you to get 30 hours in your day, which "literally" by the 24 hour clock cannot happen (we all know that).

But I promise you that you will learn some new principles, strategies and techniques, which will help you become extra productive and save you tons of time in your day.

It will start appearing to you that somehow you are able to create some extra hours in your day. These extra hours are nothing but the time saved by your conscious choices after following the principles stated in this book.

Precisely, the saved time is your earned currency, which you can spend on the things that really matter to you. It could be spending time with your loved ones, your friends, following your passion or hobbies or anything, which matters to you.

Okay! Let me guess few reasons why you are reading this book.

- You work in a corporate 9 to 5 environment or work for someone other than yourself.

- You are a small business owner struggling for more time or a freelancer wanting to deliver more and more assignments.

- You always seem to be just ticking 3-4 items out of your 15 daily to do list activities.

- You feel frustrated at the end of the day in spite of the best intention when starting in the morning to conquer the day.

- You really don't understand the reasons of why it happens to you. You are always stuck in the office till late in the evening and burning the midnight oil.

- Your spouse or beloved thinks that you are inefficient for not being able to finish your work in time, while others enjoy time after office hours.

- You seem to miss important events due to your unplanned office schedule.

- You get easily distracted over the weekend with the work you take home.

If you think, you are suffering from some or all of the above, then definitely you will not leave empty handed when you finish reading this book. With this book, I have the honest and sincere intention to deliver the maximum amount of value to you.

Okay, now you would want to tune in to the most favorite radio station in the world named WII- FM (**WHAT'S IN**

IT FOR ME). You can certainly expect many benefits from this book. A few are listed below:

- You will be surprised about how to re-wire your brain with a totally new thinking pattern towards productivity, if you implement these techniques correctly.

- You will feel like creating a few more hours in your day with simple mental and physical tweaks.

- You definitely will tick more and more items off your daily To-Do List.

- You will feel more in control of your personal and working life by creating new healthy and successful habits.

- You will take vacations without worrying about your work, as you would have already created a wonderful system to cope with your daily routine.

- You will be able to learn newer methods to implement in your daily work life.

    And many more...

I can sense your negative feeling. You must be thinking that's way too much of promise about the productivity, in this tough and challenging work environment.

Good! It is only right that you thought that way. But let me be very candid with you. I have implemented most of these techniques personally and succeeded.

The living example of implementing the productivity formula is the creation of this very book in your hands. Let me tell you that this book is written in just 4-6 weeks of consistent effort by investing morning and evening time, while doing my office day job, without compromising on my office deliverables.

SOMETHING ABOUT ME

Okay, so you must be thinking, who I am to say all those things.

First and foremost I am a regular person like you, who carries a working experience of more than one and half decades in the corporate world. During my tenure, I have worked in various types of work cultures. Be it multinational with defined systems and hierarchy or be domestic/mid-sized or consulting companies, with no limit on out-time for the office.

During all these years, I have found that there are proven methods and tips to be super productive and deliver more and more results with each passing day. Whatever kind of organizations I worked, the principles stayed with me, with minor tweaks here and there.

I have personally used these techniques, which help you to leave the office at the right time and spend time on things which matter to you.

Okay, so now you can realize that I am uniquely qualified and experienced to understand your situation, therefore I can provide the solutions to your problems.

Also, I am pretty confident to help you learn the right psychology, mindset, beliefs and healthy habits to help you improve your life in most experiential and fun way.

Okay, enough about me. Let's proceed with the book now.

HOW THIS BOOKS IS STRUCTURED

Let me explain how I have structured this book to give you a step by step blue print, which you may keep on implementing simultaneously, as you keep reading this book.

In Chapter 1 of this book, you will re-visit the definition of productivity and how you have perceived it so far in your career.

Chapter 2 will shift the gears and you will see and understand the new definition of productivity from a different perspective. You will learn about deeply rooted elements in your mind, which are responsible for changing your perception about how you can control and manage your days and life.

In Chapter 3 you will learn the macro aspects of the productivity. In fact you will turn inwards and conquer the inner game first with a new mindset, beliefs, and thinking pattern.

Chapter 4- Productivity - Micro Aspects explains that once you have mastered the inner game, it would be much easier to focus and change the action plan on the outer world. Now you can work smoothly on changing your daily actions gradually.

In Chapter 5, you will learn the importance of "Unshakeable Why" and how it is important to succeed to master the art of productivity in any area of your life.

Chapter 6 is a detailed chapter on the inner game, which focuses on explaining the 7 negative mindsets, which have held you back so far. It goes on to provide the solutions, as to how you can replace these mindsets with resourceful mindsets. It would seem simpler through deeper understanding of some core concepts and applying the easy to follow techniques.

In Chapter 7, you will learn tons of supportive habits, which you would implement in different parts of life i.e. at work, at home and in general life. This is a big one, you will enjoy learning and applying this.

Chapter 8 follows with the understanding that most of us realize that in spite of knowledge and good intentions, we end up quitting, after initial doses of motivation. So this chapter is your savior. You will learn the techniques on how to make these habits a functioning part of the rest of your life.

The last chapter (i.e. Chapter 9) gives you a 30 days challenge to master new habits in your life towards your journey to become super productive.

Okay, now enjoy your ride.

"A journey of a thousand miles begins with a single step"- Laotzu.

What is Productivity? Productivity Redefined!

What exactly do we mean by productivity?

Productivity simply means doing certain things in such a way to produce results in a time bound manner and to be able to get more things done.

The dictionary meaning of Productivity is "the effectiveness of productive effort, especially in industry, as measured in terms of the rate of output per unit of input."

WHY DO YOU NEED PRODUCTIVITY?

Why does this whole world consistently demand more and more productivity? Here are few reasons:

1. Productivity allows us to do more things in a lesser amount of time and with better results.
2. It gives you a sense of fulfillment that you were able to deliver maximum value by your work.

3. It helps you to establish a reputable image in the work place.

4. It helps you to deliver results quicker.

5. It keeps you to stay focused on the important things.

6. It could be one of the most important reasons for your promotion in your job or a steep rise in your business or profession.

7. It broadens your horizon to think on a wider perspective and to allow you to be better at what you do.

8. It boosts your confidence level immensely.

9. It allows you to spend quality time with your family, without any stress of work etc.

10. It allows you to free up lots of our time to do other activities.

As you would realize now that simply concentrating only on the one thing i.e. improving your Productivity, you will be able to achieve so many benefits.

In his book, *"The one thing"*, Gary Keller has very categorically stated that at every situation in any person's life, it is not tons of things that matter. It is really only one piece of change, which can massively improve your growth journey.

"If you chase two rabbits, you will not catch either one"- Russian Proverb

Productivity is directly connected with the effectiveness of any work you do. Here it is important to understand the difference between "efficiency" and "effectiveness".

While efficiency means doing things in a right manner, but it may or may not be that productive or effective.

On the other hand effectiveness means, in the very first place, doing only the right things, which will give you the best results.

In other words, **efficiency** refers to how well you do something, whereas **effectiveness** refers to how useful is what you do towards the objective.

For example, if your organization is not doing well and the HR Department organizes a training session on leadership and communication skills. The training goes really well - they train all the key employees in record time and tests show they have absorbed the training well. But overall productivity doesn't improve. So here the training conducted was efficient, but it wasn't effective.

So, the objective of this book is to help you become productive as well as effective in what you do in your day to day life.

Let's move next to re-define the productivity in this ever changing modern world with a new set of challenges presented before us, by understanding its relevant aspects.

Productivity Redefined...

Why do I use the phrase productivity redefined?

Let me put it straight.

Most of the material out there on enhancing your productivity solely talks about the outer part only i.e. make that list, review the list, put a tracker, make an accountability partner and so on and so forth.

It would be better to understand this with an illustration. Suppose you have a plant in your garden, which has some disease related to the leaves. If you daily take care of the leaves only i.e. by simply cleaning the dust from the leaves and don't go to the root cause of the problem, you can't even diagnose the ailment, forget about treatment and recovery.

Similarly, it is important to understand the root cause of non-productivity or lower productivity in spite of your best intentions. Once you clearly understand subjectively your problem, you are much better equipped to handle this well.

I want to give you a new definition of the productivity. It goes as follows:

Productivity means focused actions driven by a deeper understanding of the bigger purpose, which will directly and proportionately contribute to the achievement of the performer's own as well as organization's success goals.

Here I would like to give you a foolproof method which is not an objective tool, to be used by all in the same way. Rather it is a subjective tool, tailor-made for each individual' own unique purposes, which will drive one to take the requisite action towards one's goal.

Let's realize that God has created all of us differently and each of us has different priorities in life.

Therefore a "one for all" technique may help in the short term, but it doesn't give lasting results. Therefore, it is important that you should work subjectively on yourself based on your specific situation i.e. age, priorities, life circumstances, your surroundings, and your life experiences.

Following are the three key aspects to be deliberated to clearly understand the concept of Productivity Redefined.

1.   Macro Vision Lens
2.   Micro Vision Lens
3.   Unshakable Why.

In Productivity Redefined, you will make "productivity" as your end goal, but for that you will first need to clearly understand about macro vision to achieve the goal. You need to deeply realize the broad elements of your life, which makes you work in a certain way throughout almost all of your life.

You then need to understand the specifics of micro aspects. What are the precise things that need to be changed in alignment with your understanding of the macro aspects?

And last but not the least; you have to understand the deeper purpose behind everything. You need to realize that the bigger purpose of your life determines your priorities of life, which then leads to super productivity.

In the next three chapters we will dive deeper into all the three aspects. Let's keep moving.

Productivity - Macro Vision Lens

The understanding of the macro vision is the foremost pre-requisite in your journey to become a super productive person.

Macro vision in general requires us to review something from a very broad perspective like a top helicopter view. This enables us to see the complete and bigger picture of any situation.

The Macro Vision puts seemingly disjointed different pieces into a new broader perspective. Therefore, if you wish to achieve more with fewer efforts, i.e. be more productive, you have to analyze this from a Macro Vision perspective.

Following are the key constituents of Macro vision to achieve the productivity:

1.   Your Mindset
2.   Your Belief System
3.   Your Thoughts and Feelings

Let's understand what these are.

Mindset

"Whatever the mind of man can conceive and believe, it can achieve". –Napoleon Hill

So, why do you need to learn about mindset in the first place?

Here is the reason. Some of you might have already bought into this belief that this is just woo-woo stuff and doesn't work. You might have a strong belief that it is what it is and is already created. You might think that it is majorly controlled by outside situations and very difficult to change on your own.

My friend, you must read further with open and receptive mind.

You will realize, as you go further that it is the most important element towards your journey of attaining productivity in any part of your life. It has the potential of saving you years of time and money, if understood and developed correctly.

Let's understand this with an analogy!

Mindset can be compared with a computer program. The computer runs via the programs installed on it. For example, if you need to work on some imagery work, you would work with Photoshop. If you need to do some numbers work or write text, you will use MS Office i.e. MS Excel or MS Word to complete the work. Similarly, your mind is already fed with a specific set of programming into it depending upon your surroundings circumstances and life experiences so far.

What we are able to see as an output on the computer screen, is the results of the programming inside the computer. As you are reading this book in digital form, you can easily correlate. You are reading the words in the English language, but it requires a specific computer program, which delivers the desired outcome i.e. the outside view on the screen.

Since our birth, this endless programming is going on. I don't know your age, but if you are 15 or 35 or 55, while reading this, the more time you have spent on this planet, the more and more programming is written in to your mind.

Moreover, this is the irony of our world that it puts more emphasis on the "skill-set", which is more about the outer learning and experience of how to do things. On the other hand the "mindset" is something which is your own subjective perspective of looking at any particular thing or situation.

In this modern world, we are too much obsessed with outside results. But, most of us tend to disregard the fact that without the right programming inside our heads i.e. right mindset, it is almost impossible to achieve any major goal in your life.

So our mindset is like a program written in our mind, which runs our life. In the very beginning, you will find it difficult to comprehend in your head that our whole life is the result of our mindset only.

"All change is hard at first, messy in the middle and gorgeous at the end."- Robin Sharma

In your mind, you keep on believing that it is you, who is thinking like this. But as you progress in your journey, you will realize that the truth is that it is not you who decides, but in effect, it is your pre-programmed mindset, which rules your life.

This example will illustrate this better.

Compare yourself with any success icon i.e. Bill Gates, Richard Branson, Jeff Bezos (founder of Amazon.com) or any other role model in your life (No, don't think, it is too over-the-top to compare ourselves with them).

Firstly, you need to compare the physically visible similarities and dissimilarities.

You would find it funny to even think about this. But honestly speaking, you realize that their visible aspects i.e. body structure, height, skin complexion, head, arms, legs and other body parts are the same which you already possess. Physical dissimilarities are only for the specific reason that God wants each of us to have distinct separate identity.

Now, with the physical body being almost the same, what makes them so hugely successful as compared to others?

These are the invisible intangibles, which they have or developed over a period of time. You guessed right, they possess or have developed a perfect mindset to conquer all the adversities of life.

Therefore, the only difference between the super successful people and the other mediocre and failures in this world is their mindset, the computer programming in their minds, which runs their whole life on an auto-pilot basis. We make all our decisions sub-consciously based on our mindset.

And that is the reason that for the same problem, one person takes too much pressure on their mind and is unable to make any decision for a long time. Whereas, for the same problem, a matured person with an improved mindset finds a solution for immediately without any stress.

Okay, then the next question is who writes this program?

It is your surrounding environment, starting from your parents, friends and teachers to your current employment, colleagues, and bosses etc.

Now, you must be thinking if that is already created for us, then how can we improve it in a specific way.

Don't worry. You will understand in greater detail later in this book about what kind of mindsets can destroy your life and how to replace them with supportive mindset to improve your productivity. The importance of a mindset can't be undermined. Therefore, a specific chapter is dedicated to explain this with practical examples.

Now let's move to the next aspect of Macro Vision.

Belief System

The programming in our mindset is very strongly centered on our belief system. Our belief system is something, which is nurtured over a longer period of time consistently without any opposition about its correctness or usefulness.

It is so much repeated that it is almost wired in our brain and we can't even think of something different from the way we think.

An example will prove this.

When an elephant is young they are caught by circus staff. Initially they are tied with strong iron chains. There is huge resistance in the initial few days, as the young elephant wants his freedom to return back to the jungle. So he puts his best efforts in to break the chains. But after so many trials, when he is not able to break the chains, he is very much convinced that he is tied with a strong rope and there is no use in trying this.

When he stops fighting, he is then tied to a normal rope, which with the similar force, as the kid elephant applied earlier, would immediately help him to become free. But since he has time and again strengthened his belief that it is impossible to break the chain, he doesn't even try anymore. Now with this belief that it is not worth trying, he chooses to suffer an entire life of slavery.

So you can realize that beliefs are formed based on our previous good or bad experiences.

Regarding productivity also, we have similar beliefs running in our heads. You must have heard the things like.

1.   This is such an important task, how can this be completed in such a short time. You may run a test check here. The belief here is that all important decisions take a longer time. Believe me Warren Buffet, or Bill Gates don't believe this to be true for most of their important decisions, except in some big ticket items. I heard an interview and noted that Richard Branson has forged more than 300 joint ventures and makes his important decisions every time very quickly. If every decision has to take longer like weeks or months, he wouldn't have created huge empires.

2.   This work has always been done like this. Therefore, there is no other good way of doing this, so why to change, if you already have belief in your mind that it won't work. Here the deeply engrained belief is that the old way of continuing to do things is the right way, which stops us from making a change.

Let's keep moving and understand the next important aspect of the macro vision.

Thoughts and Feelings

You have to work hard to get your thinking clean to make it simple. But it's worth it in the end because once you get there, you can move mountains – Steve Jobs.

From your pre-programmed mindset and belief system, you generate the thoughts. By now it is very clear to you

25

that if your mindset is not programmed to your benefits, you will have negative or unhelpful thoughts.

We all know "Garbage in, Garbage Out".

Such thoughts will create a feeling of negativity like guilt, anger, greed, sadness, etc. You can imagine if one is thinking with a negative mindset, it leads to unproductive thinking, which further leads to non-resourceful feeling.

Guess what? With such feelings and emotions you even don't move an inch towards your goals.

So now we understand the whole equation, which moves like this.

Programming →Thoughts → Feelings → Action (or No action)

After understanding this equation, we need to really work on reverse engineering i.e. to get the desired results, we need to change our feelings. This will require positive thoughts. These will ultimately come from your programming i.e. mindset and belief system.

Productivity - Micro Vision Lens

All right, now let's understand the Productivity affecting factors through micro vision.

Micro vision unlike the macro vision is all about the things appearing outside. This is like viewing the screen of the computer, which appears as an outcome. Of course, it is true that unless you change the inner game, it is very difficult and almost impossible to see the visible results outside (except sheer luck or co-incidence only).

The following facets of micro vision are relevant to understand and improve your productivity.

Your Lifestyle

If you do what you've always done, you'll get what you've always gotten. –Tony Robbins

Lifestyle in plain words mean the style you adopt to live your life. As the micro aspects take their shape from the macro issues, so similarly, you must have chosen a lifestyle from your own circumstance, belief system etc.

A lifestyle has the potential of filling us with happiness, keep us healthy, and allow us to become more productive and successful. However, if not chosen correctly, it can adversely affect us and may lead to illness or hold us back from the things we are capable of accomplishing.

In other words, it could be a healthy lifestyle or it could be toxic lifestyle.

The examples of a healthy lifestyle could be choosing to develop a healthy relationship with family and work. Selecting healthier foods to eat and avoid junk food is another example of a healthy lifestyle.

The way you dress, the way you present yourself before others again depends upon your choice of a healthy or toxic lifestyle.

The friendship circle you have, also indicates towards your lifestyle. Are these the type of people who enjoy growing and improving their lives or do they simply complain about any or all situations and just kill time?

Lifestyles are developed over a period of time and are strongly influenced by the mindset and belief system you carry. But there is good news that we can exercise much better control on our lifestyle. And the solution towards that is disciplining you towards developing the healthy habits, which will be explained in much detail in the section on habits. Also, this is the next micro aspect.

Habits

Habit is one of the most important elements in our lives. It is what differentiates successful productive people from the crowd.

"First we make the habits and then our habits make us" - Charles C. Noble

"We are what we repeatedly do. Excellence, then is not an act, but a habit" -Aristotle

The real litmus test to check if the habit has become the integral part of your life is to gauge, if it has penetrated into your sub-conscious mind level. If the activities have become second nature to you like brushing your teeth or taking a morning bath without any conscious effort. Then you can proudly say that you have developed a habit.

Why healthy habits are important?

It is because:

"You will never change your life until you change something you do daily. The secret of your success is found in your daily routine" - John C. Maxwell

Habits need to be chosen very carefully, as there are two breeds of habits, i.e. nourishing habits and toxic habits. You will read a complete chapter on types of the habits and importance of developing the right habits. You will also learn the techniques to develop healthy habits in different areas of your life in another chapter.

Unshakeable Why - The Must

"Definiteness of purpose is the starting point of all achievement." –W. Clement Stone

If you know clearly why you want to be more productive, then how to achieve it becomes much easier and simply needs the planned action steps.

Here you must deeply imbibe in your belief system that the most important question in life is not "HOW to do" it. Rather the most important questions in life are:

1.   What do you want to achieve in life?
2.   Next most significant question- Is your "Why" strong enough to consistently keep you moving towards your "What", no matter what?

Please note that these two "Ws" are the real driving forces, which would lead one towards ultimate productivity.

So first of all you have to decide, what do you want to achieve?

Examples of your answer could be one of the following:

1.   I want to handle and successfully complete one of the most challenging assignments in the next 3 months.
2.   I want to learn a foreign language by the end of the next quarter.

3.   I want to get promoted in the next 6-9 months.

Now, these are very good examples of what you want.

But the biggest problem from these questions is that people directly jump towards as to how to achieve that. But what they forget is that the most important connecting link between "What" and "How" is "Why". You have to be very sure of why do you want, what you want.

Ascertaining your true "Why" is so important that failing might result that you were simply playing catch-up with these goals, which people around you have fixed for you (and not your authentic goals). Therefore, you must keep asking the real purposes behind each of your goal.

"Ask the right questions if you're to find the right answers." --Vanessa Redgrave

You must deeply imbibe in your veins that "Why" is your strongest motivational factor, which keeps you going in difficult times.

It is very important to understand that if you have simply put your "What" or your goals, but from the depth of your heart, you are not committed towards those goals (because of lack of "Why"), then you would take much longer to realize that this is not your true "WHAT". It would result in bad decisions.

"Clarity precedes success"- Robin Sharma

Here is a very good example of understanding the importance of true "Why", which I borrowed from one of the best books, I have read *"Compound Effect"* by Darren Hardy. The example goes like this.

If you are told to walk over a 30 feet long wooden plank lying on the ground, it is very easy to walk on it.

But if the same plank is put as a bridge on the 20th Floors between the roofs of two building, you won't think of going over there, even if someone is betting money on it. There is still no good enough reason to do it and putting your life at risk.

Now let's see how the game changes immediately by merely one tweak in the second scenario. Assume that your loved one (may be your beloved, spouse, kid or your other loved one) is standing on the other side of the plank and that building on his fire. The life of you loved one is in danger.

Suddenly, your actions change. You won't give a second thought and immediately start going over the plank to save your loved one. That is the power of the stronger why. Your Whys bring the real force behind your Whats. "How" becomes very easy and comes on its own.

So when you talk about improving your productivity, you must think about why you need it in your work life and how it will provide you with any real benefits.

Your whys might be sounding something like below:

1.   Yes, those additional hours would help me to strengthen my bonding with my family and loved ones.
2.   I would be able to be more social and uplift my spirit by being among people I like.
3.   In the saved time, I would learn one more language or some new subject or some new professional course, which would place me in better position in my life.
4.   I will join a gym or enter this year's half marathon and improve my health.
5.   I will explore the true purposes of my life.

6.   I will pursue my hobby, which I lost touch with due to a busy schedule.

You could have any type of different answer, but it is very important to find your true whys before you even think of how to accomplish them.

There is a lot of talk about the "Law of attraction" working on this principle. If you have a strong purpose for any goal, you will immediately start attracting the things, which resonates with your true "Why".

Bravo. You have come so far and understood Productivity with both a macro and micro vision. Also, you have learnt the importance of purpose in achieving any type of goals.

Now let's get to the practical stuff in the next chapter. Let's understand some of the negative mindsets and identify which bother you the most and how to replace those with nourishing mindsets.

7 Negative Mindsets, which kill Productivity and How to Replace Them Instantly

By now, you clearly understand the importance of mindset before you even think of productivity.

In this chapter, you will be able to figure out some of the limiting mindsets and beliefs, which have adversely affected your mind and thus curtailed your path to success. With this type of mindset, your actions are not decisive and will always be back and forth. These mindsets lead to a loss of your time, and even prevent you from achieving the more significant things in life.

Let's figure out, what are those mindsets and how you can easily replace them with some easy to understand techniques.

1: Perfectionist mindset

Let me be very direct here. This mindset is the major contributor, which doesn't allow you to quickly move forward towards any significant thing. With this approach, you keep on waiting until you are 100% sure that your work is perfect.

Don't take me wrong. I am not advocating that you should be compromising on the quality of the work, but the key thing is that the world is changing so fast and the universe loves speed (you can see it happening around you). The problem is that if you keep on brainstorming on any activity endlessly, someone else will move quicker. And you are left with your 'yet to be perfected' work.

You are already aware of "Paralysis by Analysis", which is caused by this perfectionist mindset.

So, the key question is: How to replace this?

The solution to this is that once your work in your judgment is 90-95% complete, then consider shipping it immediately at that point of time. With your mindset of making it 100% perfect, you will have some initial resistance, but try it a few times, it will help to overcome that perfection attitude you have.

Let's understand the concept of "shipping" fast. Shipping means to deliver your work to the right person, who needs it.

Nothing happens, until you ship.

Seth Godin-a renowned author of many best-selling books including **"Linchpin- Are You indispensable"** has greatly emphasized the need of shipping your product. Here is an excerpt from one of his blog- **The Truth about Shipping.**

"It's that little voice in the back of your head, the "but" or the "what if" that speaks up at the crucial moment and defeats the joy and insight, you brought to the project in the first place."

Read the complete blog here:

Seth's blog explains how to overcome such fears (of buts and what ifs).

Shipment is the key. Release the email, which is pending with you for endless research (not a giant life-changing, risk–it-all-venture) today and you can feel the sense of relaxation and fulfillment. Believe me, the initial fear and doubts about your self will start vanishing, after you start doing it on a faster basis.

The key question that arises here is when can you comfortable determine that it is 90-95 % done? And the reasonable answer to that is after your followed the steps stated below. If you have completed the following steps in your work, then you would be in a safer position to deliver it.

1.   Whatever your knowledge you have about the subject, you have already utilized it.
2.   You have done web research on the subject and read the available relevant material.
3.   If you have colleague working with you or under you, you have taken their views on the same and there is no disagreement.
4.   If you are surrounded by experts and the situation warrants that you have completed preliminary informal discussions with them (the experts could be your friends or it could be consultants, which you already use for your work).

So when you have done all of the above, there is simply no need to keep waiting endlessly due to your "perfectionist mindset".

I believe that this works for most of the activities done by you (I use this), though some very high stake issues may need some extra diligence i.e. detailed expert advice (but not all decisions in your work could be like this).

In most of the cases, you would be amazed to realize that your 95% judgment is recognized by the people very well. Another good point, they would realize the speed of your work now.

Okay let's move on to the next one.

2: Procrastinating mindset

You would surely agree another important hurdle, which needs to be overcome on the productivity journey is conquering the disease of procrastination.

What is procrastination?

It is nothing but simply an excuse of your mind telling you enough reasons that you can do things a bit later (even things which really matter for your growth and success), while there is no reason to delay it.

The procrastinating mindset speaks in the following languages to you. Some of the below may resonate with you:

1.   This is very important task, but this is a huge one, so I let me do it when I have enough time and when I am free from other mundane activities.
2.   How can I do this now, when I am so tired now and this is a really important job, which needs the utmost attention?
3.   Okay, let me grab a coffee and spend some time with one of my colleague doing chit chat and then I will start it.

4.   Okay this week I am too tied up with other things. Though this work is important for me, but it is better if I start this next week with a fresh mind.

5.   How can I do this alone? I would need another person's support and Jon is busy with other activities these days.

The list goes on and on and on....

But here is the thing. The procrastinating mind, which defers the important but not so exciting work always to the future, will never allow you to start the thing.

Let's talk about how to overcome that now. The quotes below really hits the nail on its head on how to address this.

"The way to get started is to quit talking and begin doing." –Walt Disney

"In any situation, the best thing you can do is the right thing; the next best thing you can do is the wrong thing; the worst thing you can do is nothing". - Theodore Roosevelt

Once you are deeply aware that this is how a procrastinating mindset operates. You would now want to learn some techniques to kill this.

Technique No. 1 - Eat That Frog.

I recommend reading the book *"Eat That Frog"* by Brian Tracy, which is really a great book to kill procrastination.

Brian Tracy in a very lucid language states that don't leave you most important thing to be done till the end of the day.

His strategy is to start your day with a difficult thing and the difficult thing is a frog. So eat that frog.

Put it simply, you must always start your day with the most important activity (even if it is very tough), even if it is not most exciting activity.

Once you start with the most important thing for you, then by the end of first half of your day, you will feel fulfilled that this big thing is either over or you have covered the substantial chunk of it.

Technique No. 2 - Lead the Horse to the water

Another tip to kill procrastination is using the technique of "lead the water to the horse". I took the liberty to take this from one of my recommended books "Vision to Reality" by Honoree Corder.

This technique simply requires you to kill the initial inertia in your mind and somehow by any means, just go and start the activity immediately, despite the initial resistance of your mind.

This technique could also be stated as the 5 minutes rules. Means that you tell yourself that you will just spend 5 minutes on this activity and if you don't feel like, you will get out of it.

Start every day with first most important activity even if it is a boring or difficult thing. There are good chances that once you start the thing and if the thing is really important, you will stick longer at it and positively will accomplish the whole or at least a substantial chunk of the work.

Technique No. 3 - Associate Punishment with procrastination.

Another one is to connect the inability to start your important project with some sort of negative stuff (i.e. punishment). For example, if I don't start this today, then I will skip one smoke break or round of coffee (mind here, the thing you choose to punish yourself with must be something you enjoy very much and wouldn't want to sacrifice).

All of this sounds funny. But believe me, your whole life is run as your circumstances have programmed it so for. Now to change your world, you have to play small tricks with your mind.

Big results are waiting for you. But remember the quote.

Think Big, Start small and Do it Now.

Technique No. 4 - How to handle the big voluminous tasks.

Rome wasn't built in a single day.

Therefore every important task takes time. But the key is consistent action.

So the question arises - How to eat the elephant?

And the simple answer is one bite at a time.

Don't get scared from the hugeness or the volume of the task.

Apply Robin's Sharma's strategy- daily improve 1% towards goal and in 30 days you will complete 30% of your work, which is a significant development.

Okay, let's move to next culprit mindset.

3: Fearful Mindset

A fearful mindset is another key dampener in your life. But you would be surprised that most of the times, you are simply scared by your own thinking without any real fear. You are afraid that the sky will fall apart, if you are not able to perform in a desired way.

This fearful mindset simply cripples you.

There could be a different kind of fear.

Fear is a necessary portion of the brain. Researchers have found that fear is established unconsciously and that the amygdala portion of the brain is involved with fear conditioning. This portion of the brain is responsible for generating fear related hormones and creating such emotions to tell you to fight or flight in some dangerous situation.

Fortunately, in the modern world, we don't have those fears of being killed in a jungle by some animal while searching for food or sleeping under a tree in the jungle.

In the modern, high tech world where we are now able to live longer, stay disease free, have access to most of the amenities for a good life, there are no such instances of fear to your life.

As stated, in most of the situations of life, there is no real fear to your life. Most often, it is your mind's own creation.

In the work environment, sometimes it is more about the fear of the person who is going to review your work. You are simply afraid that the recipient may not like this or you may not be able to fulfill his expectation.

Now let's talk about how to overcome such non-life threatening fears from your lives.

The single most important key here is to "improve your courage muscle".

What is courage?

Some feel that it is the absence of fear.

No, it is not. Rather courage is standing tall in front of your fears and still doing it.

So remember the key quote.

"Action Cures Fears" - David J. Schwartz

How do you build muscles? You build them by putting more weight, and giving more stretch to that muscle. So there is no rocket science here for the courage muscle too. But here is one most important element to keep in mind while you are on your journey to build your courage muscle.

Prepare well in advance because:

"Failing to prepare is preparing to fail"- John Wooden

Remember this quote. Put in on your desktop or paste it on wall.

Read it couple of times, while preparing for delivering the activity you fear and then just do it.

Now whenever, you get a sense of fear. Simply think that you are at gym and this is an exercise and just go in front of the fear.

It could be facing your boss in a difficult situation. It could be raising important questions in business presentations or volunteering for participation in important assignments or any other things which you fear.

"Expose yourself to your deepest fear; after that, fear has no power, and the fear of freedom shrinks and vanishes. You are free." –Jim Morrison

Here is what you would get complementary with your courageous mindset.

Small Success leads to big Victory.

Okay, let's move on to the next one.

4: Living in the Past Mindset

Most of the times, you get stuck in your mind that I have been doing this for the last 10 years or more. So you think and start believing in your head that this is the way YOU are made and so it will continue to happen like this.

No, my friend, this is not so.

Just learn this by heart:

Your past is not your future, unless you decide to make it so.

"Whatever with the past has gone, the best is always yet to come." - Lucy Larcom

Again it is your old programmed mind, which keeps on repeating the old tracks, unless you consciously change.

How to overcome this?

The strategy here is to continuously be experimenting with newer things in your life.

It could be visiting a new and different restaurant, new places to travel, meet diversely capable persons and hear their thoughts, trying different routes from your home to the office, reading versatile books, magazine etc.

The science behind this is our mind continuously runs on an auto-pilot basis based on the earlier actions, as this doesn't require additional energy of the mind. So whenever, you try newer things, you are challenging the past methods of doing those activities and you will begin to program new neuro-pathways in your mind.

Try to apply this trick several times with mind today and onwards. Do the things differently and experience your own reaction. Initially, you will feel awkward, but then you will find this interesting to follow the newer approach.

So try new things to improve your productivity.

"No problem can be solved from the same level of consciousness that created it." - Albert Einstein

So you have to improve your level of consciousness and that happens by exposing your mind to new things, new habits and new actions on a daily basis.

5: Self-worth Doubting Mindset

Here is another mindset situation, in which one keeps on doubting one's own competence and capability.

Now you can easily imagine this also has roots in the old limiting belief of bad mental programming.

Try to recall your past. It must be the case that your surroundings must have told you the stories about you not being able to do certain things.

It might be very much the case that even you yourself could be the problem. You might be your own story teller in this instance.

In such a situation, this will cause a big dent in your dreams of achieving super productivity. Every action, which you wish to complete, will get hampered by this self-doubting belief. Before attempting any significant task, you will question your capabilities and repeat the old story i.e. stopping there and not taking action.

Here is the solution. You can with some efforts easily overcome this mindset and turn this in to a super productive game.

"If you think you can do it, you are right. If you think you can't do it then also you are right". Henry Ford.

Take this challenge.

Start with small activities which don't have big repercussions, if wrongly done or in other words are capable of being reversed with very little efforts. For example, reverting to an email from a fellow colleague seeking your advice on a matter, on which you regularly work.

In this case, you need to positively affirm to yourself a few times that you are perfectly capable to do this in an efficient and effective manner. This is needed to create your new mental beliefs with the help of positive affirmations (which you will understand more in the next chapter on habits) Say this to yourself.

It is going to be easy, once I start and I can do it well and quickly.

With this affirmation, just complete this task.

Believe me; you just need 3-5 such consistent examples of succeeding in small actions, while doing the work in effective manner. And Guess what...Again compound effect works here too.

Success breeds success.

Now you are ready to take this on slightly bigger ticket items. Each success will create a new story for you.

It will take time to get in to the positive state of mind, depending upon how long you are telling the negative stories to yourself. But this is the only way and no other way.

Action is the key to success.

Okay, what's next?

6: Instant Gratification Mindset

This is another short term philosophical mindset. You must have time and again hear from people that:

1.   Life is granted only once; why not enjoy it to the fullest.
2.   You must grab all opportunities for enjoying this life to its best.
3.   And similar sounding statements.

Take an example.

You have an important project pending at your desk, which if completed in time will make you look responsible and effective in your organization. But if you choose to leave early to watch a new movie released (which you can enjoy few days later too) at the cost of work, that is called preferring instant gratification at the cost of long term benefits.

But here is the catch. When you hear these statement, you forget another set of statements (like below).

Extraordinary life takes that extra mile approach. If you think of achieving your dream, you must kick your ass off to get the massive work done at a faster pace.

There is a 10000 hours rule, which means that to attain mastery in any field of life; one has to devote 10000 hours, which comes out to be roughly 10 years. It means after putting approximately 10000 Hours to any craft and skill, you reach the level of mastery status of the specific art, craft or skill.

Listening to the first set of statement is pacifying the quench for instant gratification at the cost of the long term benefits.

Don't get me wrong. There are times, when you have to prioritize the things. If you have already spent time on the key priority items, you must reward yourself and enjoy life. Here you need to again get yourself reminded of your "Unshakable why".

You must recall how you would be able to save more time by become extra productive in your work. Imagine there is no work left on your plate (as you have turned to be more productive) and you have extra time as well to enjoy. How does that feel, great, isn't it?

"Do what is right, not what is easy." - Anonymous

Therefore, you must be willing to sacrifice at times the instant gratification to achieve the bigger benefits in your life.

7: Defensive Mindset

Another unhelpful mindset, which is big dampener of your productivity, is being defensive at your workplace. You can somehow relate this to fearful mindset. With this mindset, you do your work, but not without completely getting involved in the work. Here you simply deliver the work to the extent required and only to save your position.

It could be the case that you don't like your work or work environment. But if that is the case, you need to find solutions to change the situation within the organization or think of moving on. But taking a defensive stand might help you in the very short term, but in the longer term, you will not get rewarded in the organization, rather it would have a negative impact on your career.

You must understand that this defensive mindset will only add on to your stress. In your mind, you know that you have to do something, but you choose not to deliver intentionally.

This mindset needs to be replaced with the **"Attack or Pro-active mindset"**, if you really want to be more productive at your job.

You need to pro-actively engage with the people on whatever issues, you think may come up at your desk later. This doesn't mean to be intruding in other's work. Rather it means that getting ready for the work, which you can foresee is about to come to you.

Let me explain through the below example.

There is some deadline coming closer for some work. You know that you need input from 2 other colleagues and then only you would be able to finish that work. Therefore instead of first completing your work and then waiting for others you should start the other way round like below.

Before starting your portion, you should inform other colleagues that you are already working on your portion and request them to share their portion by a specific date. By this pro-active approach, while you are concentrating on completing your work, you have already followed up with the people to do their part, so that you are able to complete the whole project with inputs from others well in the timeframe required.

You can see that following this mindset, you will be able to always put the ball in other people's court by timely reminding and following up with them about their inputs. You can now keep focusing on your priorities, be it work, life, family or fun.

25 Best Habits - Your Ultimate Productivity Weapons

"Results can only change, when we change our consistent actions and make them a habit."- Billy Cox.

Okay, So far you have learnt about what mindsets are and the belief system, how it works and how you can replace the disastrous mindset with a productive mindset.

Once you have realized and corrected the inner world, then the next steps is implementation.

Because, the best of ideas that are not implemented are a failure, and average ideas that are implemented well are the stepping stones to success.

Therefore, now having a deeper understanding of the inner game, now it is the time to take action to unlock the true potential within you.

Fortunately, Habits help us to take actions very easily (almost on an auto-pilot basis) and make you move faster.

"We first make our habits, and then our habits make us." - John Dryden

If you really want to be productive, you have to work on developing the right set of habits. Don't' worry. It is possible, once you are committed to change your life for better.

There could be two types of habits:

Nourishing habits e.g. waking up early in the morning, eating healthy food, doing exercises, reading inspiring material, meeting successful people etc.

Toxic Habits: for example, eating junk food, watching 2-4 hours of T.V. (includes watching news for so called education purposes - (you don't need so much, really), spending quality time at work in office chit chat with colleagues. etc.

So, you have to take action in dual ways as stated below:

Increase the number of nourishing habits and reduce the number of toxic habits in your life. Or put it simply-Replace the toxic habits with the nourishing habits.

Here you need to understand the importance of the Compound Effect, which means small daily tiny actions repeated over a period of time deliver massive results.

I might be sounding repetitive, but don't forget to read the Book *"Compound Effect"*, one of the best ever books, I have read on the importance of the consistency in life.

"You will never change your life until you change something you do daily. The secret of your success is found in your daily routine"- John C. Maxwell.

Okay, now let's talk about what specific habits will reward you more specifically. I have put the nourishing habits in three categories.

Category 1 - Daily Routine Habits

1.   Wake Up Early

Why does this top the chart in your nourishing habits? There are many reasons for this.

The early morning is best suited to set the tone of your day in a positive manner. Waking up before others do, gives you time to hear your own voice (before other voices fill our day) and organize and plan your day well towards your life goals.

Your will power muscle is at its best in the morning. Your imagination and problem solving capacity is enhanced in the morning, so you need to put some time to direct this in right way.

You must have your personal morning routine, before you get dragged down in the uncontrollable events popping up during the day.

All great people have time and again emphasized the need of early rising or rising with the sun.

Robin Sharma recommends join 5 a.m. club. His slogan is "Be Wise, Early Rise"

"Success requires nothing but managing your mind and managing your day well" - Brendon Burchard

And your day always starts with mornings. So manage your mornings well.

I don't want to bulk it up here, but do some Google searching and you will notice that most of the CEOs of big corporate institutions have made the habits of waking up early in the morning. As they are already aware of the immense benefits of starting the day early, so it is part of their life.

2.   Sleep Smarter

The modern world is very dynamic. Daily, we are getting bombarded with advanced techniques and new products. It all feels overwhelming at times to consume this information in the waking hours.

We all feel the need to be on the top of all the information, be it news, be it social media or be it our subject knowledge. With all this workload, most of us tend to think that sleep is a waste of time. Don't you?

You must have heard that one third of your life you spend sleeping. If your life is 75 years, so that means, you have wasted 25 years in sleep and doing nothing.

But that is a totally negative perspective of looking at sleep.

The true perspective is to realize that only because of getting quality sleep and the right amount of sleep you will be able to productively invest your energy in your waking hours.

In his book, "*Sleep Smarter*", Shawn Stevenson explains the impact of the lack of sleep has on our brain power.

The 30 Hour Day

The research has proved that the people who tend to miss out on sleep tend to take longer in completing any task. They also tend to make more mistakes in doing their work.

The Book explains a few ways to help you get the proper sleep, so that you stay productive throughout the whole day.

1.   Reduce the exposure to any kind of light rays i.e. TV, laptop, Smartphones etc. at least 90 minutes before going to bed.

2.   Ideally, your last consumption of Caffeine in the body should be 8 hours before your sleep time. If you sleep at 10 pm, no coffee after 2 pm, as the research has proven that it reduces the quality of sleep.

3.   You must get exposure to sunlight during the day. The rays of the sun penetrate your body and give you the desired Vitamin D3. This strengthens your bones and gives you a better quality of sleep.

4.   There is so much more, in this book, if you want to learn the benefits and how to get quality sleep to improve your productivity of life.

3.   Eat and Drink Healthy Foods

How are you made?

The answer is: from the food you eat.

So it makes a lot of sense to concentrate on what you put into your body. It has been emphasized time and again that nourishing and natural food improve the brain efficiency and you become more productive.

Remember "Garbage in Garbage out"

No doubt, you will feel cravings for junk food a lot of times. You surely would want to have another slice of pizza, a can of Pepsi or another Dunkin Donut. But these processed foods make you sedentary and drain your energy when you are digesting the junk food, which leaves less energy to put to your work.

So instead of such junk food replace them with healthy salads, fresh fruits, freshly squeezed juices, milk, and raw vegetables. I am not an expert in this field, but I personally have tried and got the productive results from healthy diets by eating fresh salad, fruits, milk and dry-fruits rich in fibers.

There is enough free material available on the internet about what kind of foods will enhance your efficiency.

Also some free podcasts are really good, if you want to know more about healthy foods and other nutrition related queries. I personally like Shawn Stevenson's podcast (remember the author of the book *"Sleep Smarter"*).

http://theshawnstevensonmodel.com/podcasts/

And another very important aspect is to remember to drink lots of water each day. Lots means 8-10 liters of water every day.

The more water you consume will help to cleanse and detoxify your body and clean up your digestive system on a regular basis. Water has natural elements, which helps to dehydrate your body on a regular basis. It gives necessary quantum of oxygen to your body, which gives you the productive energy to concentrate better during your work.

Water helps to cleanse your liver and kidney and minimize the possibility of any stomach related infection. The best habit is to drink at-least 2-3 glass of water after you get out of your bed. I put two one-liter water bottles on my desk and these get filled 4 times during my office time (this is besides water consumed at home).

4.   Daily Reading Schedule

Just 15 minutes of motivational or personal development reading per day, preferably in the morning can do wonders in your life.

You already know, the job well started is half done. Same applies to your start of the day.

How reading in the morning helps?

As soon as you wake up after a full night of sleep, your mind is full of energy and not yet trapped by your routine stuff. Reading books is very much equivalent to reading the mind of the person. We must admit that most of us are not among the smartest people on this planet (I don't know about you, but I don't find myself fitting in to that category) and there are geniuses in each aspects of life. These geniuses can't be personally reached very easily, so the best means, which they make themselves available to you, is through their written word in the book form.

If you read good books in the morning, it is equal to talking to those geniuses at the start of the day. Once you make a habit of reading, this will start changing your approach in the day to day work and help you to become more productive.

Don't fret about what to read. This book contains reference to a few books, which are a good starting point.

Also, another very important tip to find the good books is to search the recommended book list (from Google of course) of your own role model.

Also, you may go to the resource section of this book, where I have given my personal recommendation of my best selected books, which you can start reading.

5.   Daily Exercise

Most of you would think how in this busy world one can still find the time to do some exercise. Come on, you are already getting late for the one and half hour of road journey to your office. You barely can even think of fitting exercise in to your schedule.

But you must recall the old saying, which is 100% true.

A Healthy mind stays only in a healthy body.

When you exercise, your body releases chemicals called endorphins. These endorphins interact with the receptors in your brain that reduce your perception of pain. Endorphins also trigger a positive feeling in the body. Therefore, exercise puts your mind in a better state for problem solving and sharpens the decision making skills.

Good news! Even if you don't have enough time, you can steal a few minutes during the day and some of them may be adjusted during your day.

Here are few tips to build in an exercise routine in your daily life.

1.   If you are on 6th floor of your office, you are quite lucky (I am). Use the stairs. Start with just getting down by stairs and then later on use them for going up as well.

The 30 Hour Day

Here you win. Without spending any extra time on a separate exercise regime or gym membership, you get some benefits. I heard on some podcast that Jeff Bezos, Amazon's founder is stated not to have used the company's elevator and uses the stairs.

2.   Use the stretching exercises, while sitting in the office. Following the YouTube video link is definitely going to help you to build an exercise routine in to your working life.

https://www.youtube.com/watch?v=vLPfP1oRJFM

3.   If you are male and shave, then you may follow this technique. When you have applied the shaving foam, during that period, say 3 minutes, do a few exercise related to the neck, arms, waist, legs etc. This is for those, who are totally short of time. And, something is better than nothing. But over the weekends, you can spend more time on the exercise.

Even if you build up a habit of doing a few minutes in a day, please don't forget the importance of the compound effect. Over a period of time, this habit will give you benefit and you would note that it has become part of your life unconsciously.

6.   Inbox Curfew – In First 1 Hour of the Day

This is a big No for anybody sincere about protecting the sanity of their minds.

The world definitely will not fall apart, if you don't see your emails the first thing in the morning.

You would say it just takes five minute to scan through your emails. Yes and No.

58

Yes, because it may take only 5 minutes or maybe less. And

NO, because it takes your attention away from more important things for a much longer period.

So if your attention has already focused on some activity, which you can do later during your day (but not now), that is a direct deviation from your morning schedule. You can't now concentrate on brainstorming your long term goals. You lose your attention to your morning self-improvement rituals and you have already trapped your attention in your inbox.

So how to avoid it- Solution- Inbox Curfew for one hour after waking up (ideally it should last till you have taken your morning bath).

7.   Meditation

To some of you, it might sound overwhelming. But the fact is that the more you relax your mind, the more productive you become.

Note that mind in a waking situation works in the Beta level. But to be in a very productive state of mind, you need to let your mind travel in Alpha waves during the day.

Meditation is the bridge or tool between the Beta and Alpha waves. There are many techniques that can put you in alpha waves. But I personally like this 3-2-1 technique of the Silva method to start with. You start with 3 and then enter into 1 through this technique.

3 stands for relaxation of physical body, number 2 leads you to mental relaxation. After that number 1 signifies the plain basic level of the mind.

I have personally experienced this technique and it gives the deepest sense of relaxation. One of the smoothest experiences of meditation, I ever had in my entire life. I have done the complete course of the "Silva Life System" and experienced immense benefits in terms of increased productivity, enhanced mental focus, easy to incorporate and quicker techniques (less than a minute even) to get the deepest relaxation of mind even during the busiest days.

Therefore I strongly recommend you to experience the centering technique, which is freely available.

But one precaution here!

Please don't make quick judgments based on your pre-conditioned mind. Do it with an open mind and some faith that it will benefit you and then continue to do it for at least the next 10 days. You will find great relief from stress, improve your focus and become more productive throughout the whole day.

Here is the link to the Free "Centering technique"
http://www.silvalifesystem.com/free-lessons

8.   Positive Affirmations - A new way

"Whatever we plant in our subconscious mind and nourish with repetition and emotion will one day become a reality." - Earl Nightingale

If you have watched the movie *"Secret"* or read the book *"Secret"*, you must have noticed the importance and significance of positive affirmations.

Affirmations are precisely a set of statements, which you repeat consistently in your mind to impress upon your sub-conscious mind a new set of beliefs to direct you towards positive living.

This is important because your mind is bombarded daily with all sort of negative statements, some from your family, from your colleagues, from the media crying about the state of the economy, crime news etc. Whether you believe it or not, all such information is very subtly impacting your mind in a negative manner.

Here, positive Affirmations play a vital role in nullifying the impact of all those negative statements and if consistently repeated over a period of time, it impacts your subconscious mind significantly. It re-wires your brain for positivity and success.

But here is a big problem for most of you.

Affirmations traditionally have been explained as the positive statement stated in such a manner that you have already achieved your desired state in the present tense.

But for some of you, you would feel that stating something in your mind which is not the actual situation might seem like making fool of yourself.

Take this example of a positive affirmation.

I am very productive and I handle the things very actively and in a consistent manner.

If you are actually not experiencing such a state of productivity, then while stating this affirmation to yourself may sound like making fool of yourself.

I personally couldn't believe this for a long time for the above reasons. It also took me few years to trust if this really works and luckily then I stumbled across one of the refined techniques

Hal Elrod in his best seller book *"Miracle Morning"* teaches a different way of positive affirmation. This seemed to be a more realistic and practical approach towards using affirmation in your life.

What do you think of below example of affirmation?

1.   I am committed to massively improve my productivity throughout the whole day.
2.   I am committed to massively improve my confidence and courage to stand tall in front of all fears.

Don't you think, these seem better, as you acknowledge your commitment to develop on a daily basis, as compared to previous statements, in which case you felt like telling a lie to yourself?

The best result, you can get is in front of the mirror with your emotions and again no quick judgment. Every new technique takes time and here you are trying to make tricks with your brain (which is already pre-programmed in the old manner).

Okay now we move on to specific work place habits to enhance your productive instantly in your working day.

Category 2: Work Place Habits

9.   Never Argue or Complain:

You would not realize how much time we all generally waste in ranting about the small issues in our home, office, public places, road, shops etc.

The problem with complaining or arguing is two-fold.

Firstly, you are wasting too much time whilst arguing and complaining on certain things, which probably are out of your control, so you can't do much about that. For example a traffic jam, the sudden pressure of additional work coming from your boss, etc.

But second the most important problem with complaining is that it steals your attention to a large extent, even when the useless ranting session is over. Now with this negative mindset, you waste another couple of hours thinking about the same thing.

So now you have to replace your "complaining" habit with a "solutions" habit.

To make the solution habit your friend, let's put each and every situation you come across in two categories. Whether the situation is under your control or not?

If not, then simply leave it then and there, just delete it from your mind.

If the situation is under your control totally or partially, then take immediate action on that.

In his book, *Miracle Morning*, Hal Elrod emphasizes on this "Accept the reality as it is (the things, which you don't have control on) and focus on what you can change".

This mindset only, is going to save you tons of time. The productivity is enhanced. And a few more hours released in your day. Cheers.

10.   Inbox Management Habits

Another principle to remember is too much concentration on the inbox is making you slave of other people.

"The inbox is nothing but a convenient organizing system of other people's priorities" -Brendon Burchard.

There are a few principles for managing you inbox management, which can help you improve productivity and save your much time:

1.   Don't start working on the email immediately, when it comes in. Rather dedicate a pre-determined time slot(s) for reviewing your emails. Read emails in batches. May be 3-4 different time slots during the day and then keep prioritizing during the day, depending on the importance of the matter.

2.   You may open a 'sticky note' or 'notepad' on your computer and just put it in your to-do-list to review later, so you don't forget.

3.   Don't stress too much on email, when you can't take immediate action.

4.   Another important aspect is don't look at the email at certain times, when you are not in a position to do anything I.e. checking your blackberry at 10 pm in the night (unless some important assignment is going on). The reason being is that if you can't handle them at that time, it simply is taking your unnecessary attention, which will disturb your sleep and spoil your next day's productivity.

So the principle is that if you are going to the office tomorrow morning then you can work on that tomorrow morning, don't allow your attention digress from the present activities. Use that time to relax and in the morning, you may pay full attention to all such activities in the office.

It takes a lot less time to check the email. But it takes a lot of your attention for lot more time, in which you can't do anything about that.

Besides the above principles of managing the inbox, you may follow one technique of using your inbox to your best advantages.

In this technique, after you have identified your priorities or to-do-list at the start of the day, you just focus for those items, in which you need some inputs from other colleagues. After figuring them out, use the inbox to your advantage, by sending required emails to other colleagues in one batch time slot, so you can get the required information for your work at the later stages. This will keep other people busy in the work, you required of them. In that period, you can focus on your own work.

Sounds simple, isn't it?

11.   Meetings Habits - How to effectively handle

"Meetings are indispensable when you don't want to do anything." - John Kenneth Galbraith

In the modern corporate world most of the decisions are the joint decisions to be taken by the management. So this creates the requirement of sitting together to discuss.

But, you must have observed some of the meetings (not all) turn out to be unproductive, as people get distracted from the main agenda to other side issues. It also happens that meetings (indirectly) happen in such a way for jointly agreeing to not taking further action under the disguise of further brainstorming, which might look to you not in the best interests of the organization.

Since, meetings will continue to remain the necessary evils for at least some time in the future, you need to be mindful that you simply don't get trapped in such time-wasting meetings. Primarily, in your efforts to improve productivity, you must adhere to some rules for attending the meetings:

1.   First and foremost, just sense with the topic of meeting, if it is really important for your function or you are just being invited for your views. In the latter case, try to avoid the meeting, unless you have to attend. The following statements can help you avoid attending such time wasting meetings.

a.   Sorry, I have got another call starting in the next 10 minutes
b.   I have really lots of deliverable during the day, so I will get the de-briefing from other colleagues after the meeting.
c.   Whatever is required from me as my view, I have already shared/will share via email, as I have other commitments at your schedule time for the meeting.

2.   In urgent and important meetings, please go fully prepared with all the contents from your side.
3.   If you are hosting the meeting, please communicate well in advance to all the people, as to what is expected from each of the attendees and request them to come with preparation on the agenda.

4.   If you see that the meeting is dragging on too long, without any significant progress, get out of the meeting to handle other things. Be careful to get out smartly, so others don't feel offended. You may have another call or meeting scheduled, which you can inform to the group.

12.   Prioritize vs. Time management

Obviously, all of us get the same 24 hours in a day and one third of the day goes into rebuilding our bodies and mind (sleeping). So effectively, we are left with only 16 hours in a day.

So your goal here is to squeeze those 16 hours to the best of your abilities. That's what successful CEOs and entrepreneurs do. But how do we do it?

It is simple, but not easy.

Time management is BS. It is based on a flaw that everything on the list needs to be ticked off in some timeframe, whereas the fact is that you must memorize by heart every situation of your life. There are only very few things that really matter the most.

The mantra is to prioritize. Your question to you should be- What is the one thing, if I do it now that will make all the other things super easy to complete or become unnecessary.

So here is the way to do it.

Ask yourself every 2 hours (or less, depending upon the size of your project in hand), is it the best use of my time as of now.

I personally had put the following reminders in my desk based on the advice of Tim Feriss- the author of the best-selling book- *"The Four Hour Work Week"*. Though, I don't personally follow with all the points covered in the book, but few points are worth implementing including this reminder technique.

1.   "Am I being productive or simply active"
2.   "Am I inventing things to do to avoid the important"

These reminders will continuously remind you to prioritize your work in hand. I put these on my MS Outlook calendar 2 times a day for a long time, which constantly reminded me to get back to my important work.

But in what order do you prioritize the work. Unless you already are habitual of prioritizing the work in some manner here is the way, you can also think to prioritize (I follow this).

Your prioritization should be on the following parameters.

1.   The first priority would always be to act on your immediate reporting managers' requirement (unless you get some work directly from your Reporting manager's boss, which then becomes the first one). Your job is to make your boss look good in front of all.
2.   Your colleagues from different departments, who are seniors to your reporting managers.
3.   Your colleagues, who help you in your work at short notice and respect you, so reciprocate.
4.   Any other thing, which in your view is very important to the organization and you think worth informing management about. Please do this and route it

through your reporting manager only (preferably in all cases).

5.   Forget everything else. Yes, you heard this right. Avoid all other work, until you tick off all the above top priorities. Please remember that there will always be people, who will complain. It is the nature of the world. Let them do so. Time is your limited and precious resource. Use it wisely to get the maximum amount of benefit out of it.

13.   Pareto Principle

The Pareto principle was formulated after the name of the Italian economist Vilfredo Pareto in 1906. This principle is also known as 80:20 Principle. It simply states that the world works around the principle that only 20% of your activities (even lesser) are as important to deliver to you as the 80% results (even more) in your life. It could be substantiated by following facts:

1.   99% of the World's wealth is accumulated by only 1% of the people.
2.   80% or more of every business's turnover/profits are contributed by only 20% or less of its customers.
3.   If you satisfy 20% of the people in your life with your work, that will give you an 80% assurance of the perfect working life.
4.   The list can still go on...

To be productive and effective in discharging your job, you need to consistently watch your to-do list.

You must apply the Pareto principle. You have to scrutinize all the activities and ascertain what 20% of the activities, if you invest time on, have the potential to deliver you the 80% of your results. You already know the general principle of prioritizing in the previous point.

The best book to understand this principle, if you want to dig deeper into this is **The 80/20 Principle: The Secret to Achieving More with Less by Richard Koch**

14.   Parkinson's principle

Another very important principle is Parkinson's Law, which states that the lesser the time you earmark for some activity, the more effectively you handle that activity. There is every chance that you would have already experienced this in your real life.

Imagine you had an exam or an interview or a new customer meeting, which was scheduled to be held three weeks later. Suddenly, you get an email or phone call or message that said the event is to happen next week.

Now what is your initial reaction (mind it, it will vary from person to person). It could be a scary feeling or thoughts of frustration, anxiety etc. on such a sudden change. You might feel overwhelmed with the volume of work still left to be done for that important event.

But in most of the cases, the truth is that if that event is really important and a matter for your success, you work pretty smartly to address the situation in the shorter timeframe. The key message here is that your mind adapts to the changes and works according to the situation.

Now the practice step for you is to allocate reasonably stretched timelines to achieve the same goal. This will help you strengthen your mind muscle. You will get some tools in this book in the later chapters to implement this.

15. Combine Pareto with Parkinson - see the explosion in productivity.

Now you understand the Pareto's and Parkinson's principle. Let's talk the next big thing and you will be surprised to see the rise in your work productivity. Yes, use Pareto with Parkinson in a combined manner and see the explosion in productivity.

Firstly realize that Less is more (80:20 Principle) and then also try to achieve "More (work) with Less (time)".

You are doing only the most important things and as such you are giving your mind a good stretch to do it in a shorter time.

Shorter time to complete any work enhances the total focus on that very thing. Our mind is also muscle, the more you challenge it, the more it will grow. Remember, we only utilize 10% of our mind.

16. Principle of 4Ds - Decide quickly either to Do it, Defer it, Delegate or Delete it

This is the important rule to be remembered every time, you start doing some work. There could be only a few categories in which any kind of work needs to be created immediately.

Do it now. If it meets the priority criterion explained earlier.

Defer it - Defer it to a later time depending upon the level of prioritization.

Delegate it - if you think, the work doesn't require specialized expertise of your level and other person can do it then delegate this.

Delete it - All the work coming to your desk needn't be done. Some emails may be simply ignored, as they don't fit into your priority work list at all.

If you keep on thinking for a long time about assigning either of the "D" to any specific work, then you are inviting trouble, as the work will keep on piling up. So whenever you are taking stock of the items earmark either of the four "D" on the item and just keep moving.

Whatever "D" you mark, be sure to perform that. Regarding "delegate", please categorically make sure that you are delegating only that work, which you totally understand.

Don't ever delegate the work to someone that cannot complete the work. You will create a mess of it.

Let's move to the next one.

17.   Apply STOP Principle:

This is another Principle, which is very helpful in taking thoughtful and quicker decisions. As you would realize that merely rushing, but leading in wrong direction (due to hurry) will take you much longer to return from the wrong path back to the right path. Besides, it adversely affects you motivation and will power.

Here the STOP principle will help in most of the cases.

STOP stands for

S - Stop

T - Think

O - Option

P - Proceed.

There is no guarantee for each time. But the better decisions you make, the more confident you will be and then this will create a 'snowball effect'.

So, you already know how to implement this. Sounds simple. "Captain Obvious", isn't it?

So whenever you come across any situation, where you have to make a decision. Follow this four step formula:

1. Stop and don't react immediately
2. Think about the problem and if required break it into sub-problems (remember controllable and non-controllable)
3. Now consider the options available in the case of a controllable situation (under your control somehow, by your efforts).
4. Proceed, only when you have considered all the available options. You will be able to proceed faster, once you have considered the problem and spend time on seeing the options.

One precaution! Since I have written in so many words that doesn't mean that it should take ages to apply the STOP principle.

You would realize that some situation may require immediate action, so in such cases, you have to implement the STOP process immediately.

Don't ever get plagued with paralysis by analysis. Using this principle, go ahead with what is the basis of your own best judgment.

18. Make distinctions between Mistake or blunder.

A person who never made a mistake never tried anything new - Albert Einstein

To err is human. A mistake also indicates that the person is doing some work.

Committing a mistake is not bad in itself. There are few things worth noting about the mistakes.

To make a mistake is not bad, unless it is for the first time and in a new area, you haven't worked in previously.

Mistakes are also okay; so far as you don't foresee that it leads to a blunder. Remember, all mistakes don't lead to blunders.

The difference between a mistake and blunder are:

1.   Mistakes generally have small adverse implications, blunders have bigger ones.
2.   The impact of mistakes can be reversed by some corrective actions, but blunders are very difficult to recoup without heavy investment of time and money.

So you have to be action oriented and simply use your judgment that mistakes should not lead to a blunder. With that precaution, you can improve the speed of your deliverables. Read Einstein's quote again here.

A person who never made a mistake never tried anything new - Albert Einstein

It is also important to realize that mistakes can be of your own or of others making. You don't need to be responsible for all the mistakes (life is too short for that).

You can reduce your journey much shorter, if you learn from other peoples mistakes.

Don't ask how to find the mistakes of others. Remember the habit of Daily Morning Reading and you can easily find the resources or books on whatever you want to learn. The successful people have generally the habit of sharing their failures on the way, so others can learn from those mistakes or failures.

Okay, let's move on to the next category of Habits.

Category 3: General Life Habits:

19.   Intuition

"The intuitive mind is a sacred gift and the rational mind is a faithful servant. We have created a society that honors the servant and has forgotten the gift" - Albert Einstein

Do you sometime realize and state the words, my Gut feelings say this or that. This gut feeling is called intuition. Intuition is something, which connects you with the supreme power (governing all of us) and helps you to assess the situation.

All great people, who are able to take the right decision at the right times at a faster pace in their lives, when the world was laughing at them, have the habit of relying on their gut feeling. They move in spite of fear of any sort (fear of negative outcome, people rejection, or fear of self-worth doubt), if their gut says to move further.

I heard some podcast and surprised to learn about Richard Branson's (who has more than 300 business brands in his kitty with his joint venture partners) intuitive skills. He is stated to be able to judge within 60 seconds of shaking hands with a complete stranger if that person is worth doing business with or not.

Let's get deeper into what "Intuition" is.

Intuition literally means "Inner Teacher". Intuition doesn't come from your mind; it comes from your heart.

Do you know the heart is a thousand times more intelligent an organ than your mind? The heart develops much earlier than your mind, whilst in your mother's womb. But in modern societies, we are literally bombarded with logics and reasoning, that we have stopped using intuition at all. There are so much layers of dust put on our intuition that we even don't realize that it exists for all of us.

But the fact is whenever, you disregard intuition, you are ignoring the signals released to you for your best purposes in life. Unknowingly, to our disadvantage, we keep on thinking that it is a born skill and not everyone can attain this.

So, how to do you activate and use the intuition to make the best decisions in your life?

It takes time to practice and implement this.

You can try this simple tip that whenever, you come across a situation of taking some decision, stop and listen to your heart. If one of the alternatives gives you a better feeling in your heart and stomach area, then go with that.

In some decisions, there might be a feeling of uneasiness or discomfort in moving further. In such cases, you might probably reconsider this. Sometimes there might be only the fear of moving further, but don't fool yourself in such cases that your intuition is stopping you to move ahead (rather, not moving ahead may give you a bad feeling). Depending upon how developed your intuitive skills are, you would be able to take decisions in your life.

Steve Jobs is stated to be one of the most intuitive of people, who could use his intuition to believe that people would prefer touch instead of pushing buttons, so we have the Iphones, Ipads, which have now revolutionized our world. Read what he thinks about intuition:

"Your time is limited, so don't waste it living someone else's life. Don't be trapped by dogma - which is living with the results of other people's thinking. Don't let the noise of others' opinions drown out your inner voice. And most important, have the courage to follow your heart and intuition. They somehow already know what you truly want to become." – Steve Jobs.

Since this is not the core subject of this book, but one of the sub-topics to understand better. I personally enjoyed doing the course "Tune In" by Sonia Chouquette and don't hesitate (rather feel proud) to recommend to people to go through this course for improving their intuition muscle.

For a brief introduction on the intuition journey with Sonia, just click the link below.

http://www.positiveintuition.com/products/special

20.　Develop Emotional Intelligence

We all know and talk a lot about Intelligence Quotient (IQ). Bill Gates is stated to have an IQ of 160, which is considered very high.

But the researchers have now proved that Emotional intelligence (EQ) is 3 times more powerful and gives the results as compared to your IQ and talents compared together.

Understand and improving our EQ is comparatively less talked about subject as compared to IQ. But it is very important to stay super productive for longer times at our work and other areas of life.

See, we are human beings and when we talk about productivity, we surely cannot work like machines.

We have special traits of emotions in all of us. These could be the emotions of anger, depression, greed and other negative emotions.

Therefore let me put it in a simple and very straightforward manner.

Your entire success or failure depends on your emotional intelligence in handling the situation and challenges of your life.

You would have seen the most talented people, in their moments of adversities get trapped in the emotional dilemma. With such emotional behavior, they do such activities, for which they suffer for a long time.

Every day we see people taking self-damaging actions by getting trapped in the momentary emotional situation. All the prisoners filled in the world prisons are not the dumb or wrong persons, some of them just took the wrong actions due to a lack of not controlling their emotions at the right time.

Would you want a few Mantras to develop your emotional intelligence? Would you want to make this a part of you daily habits?

I can hear the answer from you.

It is a resounding "Yes", right?

Below are a few statements, if you could fit it into your mental programming and change your mindset and belief system, will help you to be more emotionally intelligent and thus improve your day to day actions.

The wise men immediately realize, what are controllable things and what are not. They don't even react on the things, which are outside their control, instead they massively focus on what is in their control and what they can change.

"Accept the Reality as it is (things not in your control), and Focus on what you can Change"- Hal Elrod

Here is an example.

Imagine you couldn't fully deliver on one project and have to face the repercussion of annoyance from your superior.

Here's what you can (or rather should do from an EQ perspective) do?

You should immediately accept it and feel in your mind that you can't change the past now. So there is no use getting depressed and worrying yourself about the past.

The best action is to immediately take steps to control the situation. You could explain that the project is almost complete. You could say, that in its present form, the project could be used to some extent. You should request an extension on the deadline to allow you that extra time to allow you to put as much effort as possible in to delivering the project. The thing is you can only take action on things that are under your control.

Hope you see the difference in the approach.

Here are some of the techniques to develop your Emotional Intelligence muscles.

A: Commit you not to take anything personally

Please remember this lesson because it will save you most of the fights (outside and inside).

Read this carefully.

Not all the other people's talk and opinions about you are the truth.

There will only be a few people that will be your true well-wishers and give you the best advice. Others either may not be competent enough to express an opinion about you or they maybe the type of person that just likes to spread gossip and just say anything about anyone (so why bother about them at all).

So to start with, you must be sure of only the very few people who are honest about you and you must learn from their feedback. For all other the people, you have to develop a rhinoceros skin and not take their criticism personally.

There are no reasons to react to the second category of people. As it will only depress you and will have a negative impact on your productivity. Just use the feedback or advice from your trusted few and move towards things which you can change.

B: Always replace your judgments with sympathy

Okay, this is another powerful technique that will help you to control your emotions.

It may be hard to believe, but the fact of the matter is that all your feelings about any person or situation are generated based on your judgment about that person as per your belief.

If you pre-judge any person or situation to be adverse, you will accordingly react in a not so good way, and it may cause a ripple effect.

However, if you stay open minded and don't be judgmental or quick in making a conclusion about any person, you will be conscious of taking into account all the other parameters, then you will react differently.

Here is an example.

When your reporting manager is in bad mood, and if you replace your judgment about him/her with sympathy, then you would try to understand them better and take actions accordingly.

I know, it might sound absurd to some people. But you must understand that the way you have emotions, the other person also has the ability to be emotional.

"We judge ourselves by our intentions and others by their behavior." — Stephen M.R. Covey

So the best solution to this is to replace your judgments of any sort with sympathy (i.e. try to understand the other persons situation for any specific behavior). Don't make any kind of judgments (adverse judgment, not at all) and whenever any thought comes, replace that with sympathy towards the person.

C: Everything is difficult before it becomes easy, every experience is uncomfortable before it becomes comfortable.

This statement, if you can embed in your mind, is going to serve you for life.

It is a new set of beliefs. With this belief, you automatically generate a vibration in your mind and heart that this is definitely going to be easy over the course of time, so you stick to your action.

With this belief, you would perceive every uncomfortable situation as if it will just pass by. If you have that belief, then you will venture into most of the activities very positively and have a much better chance of success.

With utmost positive hopes that it is merely initial hiccups or hurdles, then the way you start and handle any issue becomes totally different. You develop a stronger faith that things will get easier, as you progress, so you concentrate on taking action and actions breeds confidence and delivers results.

21.   Be a Learning Machine

"Knowledge is power. Information is liberating. Education is the premise of progress, in every society, in every family "- Kofi Annan

If you wish to really want to be successful in life, then keep building your knowledge in your chosen field at all opportunities.

This one short story will help you to understand this better.

There were two woodcutters who stayed in the jungle. One woodcutter used to spend the whole day in the jungle and returned home tired with a small quantity of wood in his bundle, in spite of his hard work, let's call him the Poor Guy. But another woodcutter would simply go for just a couple of hours in the forest and would bring back a larger quantity of wood by doing less work. He did this on regular basis. Let's call him the Smart Guy.

The days passed by and the Smart Guy got richer with the least amount of effort. The Poor Guy was barely able to make both ends meet. After a long wait, The Poor Guy couldn't hold himself back and reached out to the Smart Guy to learn the techniques of his super productivity and success with the least amount of effort.

The Smart Guy was generous and was pleased to share the reasons without holding anything back.

He stated that the reasons he could spend less time in the forest and still cut more wood was very simple. He told that he spent the maximum number of hours sharpening his axe and used that sharpened axe for just a couple of hours and cut more wood.

The Poor Guy was simply amazed with this simple principle, just like you are feeling now.

So the moral is, if you put more efforts in to sharpening your mind, you will be able to get more rewards in resolving the bigger challenges and improve your overall productivity.

Always try to learn newer techniques to enhance your capabilities.

Here are the few ways, you can improve your learning, even if you are short of time.

A. University on wheels

I learned this term from Brian Tracy. You can't complain about the shortage of time here, because you are just wasting time already, which can be best utilized.

He states that if you fill your car with full of educational audio material. Don't listen to stupid songs etc. (sometime for a change this is fine). This is the best utilization of your time, as you can't do anything else while driving the vehicle.

Nowadays, there are so many audio podcasts on all different kinds of subject i.e. on personal development, habit formation, finance, starting a business etc. You can find a podcast on almost any subject. Make your car a University on wheels.

B. Online educational website to MOOC

Nowadays there is an online concept called Massive Open Online Course (MOOC). There are lots of free material and courses available on these MOOC websites. Just search Google to find them.

www.Udemy.com offers very well designed and structured courses on different subjects. They are sometimes free as well as low priced. This type of course allows you to learn in the comfort of your own home.

You don't need to travel anywhere to attend any physical classes or courses. You don't need to spend a large amount of money to learn any new skill. Therefore, there is no excuse for you these days.

C. Attend seminars

Another good way to learn is to attend seminars that are conducted by the best people in the industry on the skills you need to learn.

You must realize that there are different ways of learning. Unlike books, which you have to read, they don't speak to you. Attending conference gives you multiple benefits as follows:

1.   Firstly, you get the latest available information. The professional speaker is telling it to you in the present form, so no obsolete or old information.
2.   You get the opportunity to directly clarify your queries/question at the same time from the person.
3.   You get a whole environment full of people who have come with the similar objective as you i.e. learning.
4.   This is a good place to network. Who knows, you may find you next business partner or best friend meeting you at this forum.

While learning, please always keep in the mind the principle.

"Learn from the best people in the field".

This cuts your learning journey very short and makes your success path comparatively much easier.
Remember learning from the mistakes of others (meaning successful others).

D. Speed Reading

This habit has the potential to massively improve your productivity.

As you are a knowledge worker, which I presume because you are reading this book, then you must concentrate on speed reading courses.

In fact, Bill Gates, who is a voracious reader, was once asked what superpower he most wanted. Guess what he chose?

"Being able to read superfast" he answered.

Though he already reads at a very fast pace and has read tons of books. See the books collection of Bill gates on his personal blog.

http://www.gatesnotes.com/Books

Read this very helpful blog post on speed reading by Tim Ferris, author of best-selling book - *Four Hour work week.*

Scientific Speed Reading: How to Read 300% Faster in 20 Minutes

http://fourhourworkweek.com/2009/07/30/speed-reading-and-accelerated-learning/

The Truth About Speed Reading

http://lifehacker.com/the-truth-about-speed-reading-1542508398

Let's move to next topic about general habits.

22. Be Smart, Use effective Smartphone Habits

Smartphone! Very rightly coined name!

It really makes you smart, if you choose well. Hope you already possess one. If not, grab one immediately. With a smartphone, you can carry a lot of educational stuff at your fingertips. Here are some of the resources you can utilize on your smartphones, while on the go.

1.   E-books on kindle, ibooks and other online published material.
2.   Audio podcasts containing tons of informative interviews of successful people.
3.   Audio Books.
4.   Endless mobile apps to enhance your productivity.

There are plenty of mobile apps, which I have covered in this book in the later chapter, which you would find useful.

23. Identify and emphasize on your strengths

Someone has rightly stated:

"Invest in your strengths and these will grow you exponentially and try to improve too much on your weaknesses will make you only mediocre."

So the most important challenge before you is to identify your strengths and then work on those strengths.

There is a quick tool with an exercise, which would really help you to understand your strengths.

Apply the principle of prioritization here. You should prioritize to improve your strengths and do fix your weaknesses only to the extent that is required.

This free exercise here (little longer) is worth exploring your top strengths.

http://freestrengthstest.workuno.com/

24. Replace Television with Internet

You and I are very fortunate to live in this modern world with daily new inventions. The Internet is the key invention, which has changed the way we perceive and understand the world today.

I personally don't watch TV (except 30 minutes to 1 hour a week in total) and consider this as one of the time wasting activities.

Some people watch the TV serials or reality shows. Some people spend much of their time watching the news on TV. The second category would say that they are enhancing their knowledge.

Here is an important thing to note.

The TV serials/news don't know what exactly you like or dislike. It is made for everyone and relayed at specific times. They don't give you the freedom to exercise your discretion to watch a specific thing (of course you change the channels and see the different programs). Media generally has the habit of only telling the brief story for a long extended period, thanks to 24/7 news channels.

The best advice here is to replace the TV with the Internet. By doing that you will become in-charge of the information consumption at your will. This will give you total control of whatever you want to watch, and also how long you want to watch it.

Specifically coming to the daily news! It would sound blunt, but let me tell you that the world is not operated by your watching the news. It is already going on. To become a well-informed person, surely you need to be aware about your surroundings, but I am sure that it never requires two hours of TV watching every day.

It might be better for you to watch YouTube or any other internet news channel and dedicate 15-20 minutes daily to surf through the news and select the long reads for later consumption. This will go a long way in helping you in your career advancement.

25.   Change your association

"You are the average of the five people you spend the most time with." — Jim Rohn

Yes, my friend, your company or associations really defines you and determines the way you take action on a day to day basis.

Therefore, you need to really do a self-assessment to see what kind of people you are surrounded with during your work time. What kind of friends do you meet in the evening and over the weekend? What kind of habits, your circle of influence possess?

Brendon Burchard in his book *"The Charge"* strongly insists on finding and cultivating the 'growth friends'.

This means the people whose company inspires you to think big and grow in life.

In this super connected world, it is very easy to find like-minded people.

One very significant tool to start meeting people is to join www.meetup.com. This site helps you to join already created meet ups and you may also create your own new Meet-up Group. The topics could be anything you can imagine i.e. book lovers, marathoners group, start-ups, simply coffee meet-ups and so on.

Nothing happens in a day. Of course it will take some time, but working on building new and growth oriented connections will re-wire your brain and you will think and act differently. And you know very well by now that productivity is all generated from a positive and clear mindset.

How to form Habits Quickly- 8 Simple but Effective Tricks

"Knowing is not enough, we must apply. Willing is not enough, we must do." — Bruce Lee

Okay, you have really come a long way to understand about the different types of bad mindsets and how to replace them with the healthy mindsets, so you can benefit.

You also now know that the habits you have make your action plan towards productivity very easy and achievable and almost on an auto-pilot basis.

Therefore now the key action plan for you is to discipline yourself towards creation of new and positive habits.

This chapter is a practical chapter and you will learn certain techniques or tips on how to form the new habits.

66 days Principle:

Research has proven that it takes 66 days to build any new habit in your life. Building any habit means that it should happen in your life like brushing your teeth daily i.e. it should happen at the level of your sub-conscious mind. Earlier theories of 21 days or 30 days don't really give the long lasting impact and it is now established that it takes 66 days to form any new habit.

So you have to tighten your belt and get ready to develop the resourceful habits. This will not be too difficult, if you keep reminding yourself of your "unshakable why" and the principle of "compound effect".

You must stick to it for 66 days to form any habit. It is not the case that only on day 66, the magic will happen. You will gradually start seeing the improvements during this practice period. The initial week or two would be challenging, as you are breaking the old habits, followed by some feeling of discomfort in the next couple of weeks. But as you keep going, it will start becoming easier.

The additional benefit is a drastic improvement in your confidence that "you can do it", which will replicate in all other areas of your life.

Importance of Discipline

You know the importance of discipline in your life. But that doesn't mean that you should grill your entire life by discipline.

Don't jump from your chair when I say - You don't need to be disciplined for your entire life.

Yes, that's right.

You need discipline only when you need to form a new habit. This is because once, with the help of your discipline, you have formed a habit, then further discipline is not required. The habit will begin to take over and will automatically be programmed into your sub-conscious mind without any further resistance.

Reduce the scope, but stick to the schedule.

In the initial 66 days, you will come across tough days, shortage of time, office travel, too much work, and the kids getting sick and other pressing reasons. So how do you stick to 66 days, with the uncertainties or unpredictable events coming along in life?

There is a trick, which we call "reduce the scope and stick to the schedule".

So what you need to do is to just do a very brief version of your habit, but stick to the schedule. Suppose you daily want to walk up 10 flights of stairs, but in urgent times, you may only go up 2-3 floors and use the elevator for remaining 7 floors etc.

Bring the horse to the water.

I read the book *"Vision to Reality"* by Honoree Corder and borrowed this technique of bringing the horse to the water in habit formation. What it precisely means is that when you don't feel like sticking to habits just use the following technique.

You say to yourself that I will just show up at the required time for the activity, even if I don't feel like.

Suppose you promise yourself to go to the gym 4 days in week and then one day you don't feel like going. In such a case, just go to the gym and do just a few exercises, but do it. In extreme cases, you simple show up at the gym without even doing any exercise. After a few times, your mind will start adapting to the new pattern.

This is also called the 5 minute rule (i.e. you tell yourself that I will do it only for five minutes). In most of the cases, once started, you will complete your routine.

Easy vs. Difficult manipulation:

Make the implementation of good habits easier and the following of the bad habits tougher for you.

One of the interesting tricks on your mind to form a new habit is to engineer your circumstance in a different manner. Let's understand it by an example.

If you want to cut down your TV watching time drastically, then do the following.

Remove the power cord of the TV from the electricity supply. Also remove your cable connection from the plug. The idea is to make the continuation of bad habit difficult.

Regarding developing good habit, you need to do the reverse (i.e. make it easy). For example, you want to go jogging every morning. Then you need to put your track suit, jogger shoes in the right place the night before, so in the morning, you find it super easy to do this.

Engineering Atmosphere

Here you need to engineer your atmosphere towards new habit formation. For example, let's assume that you want to develop the habit of taking a healthier breakfast full of fruits or raw vegetable or milk. But you are not able to control your cravings for 6 cups of coffee, hot chocolate etc. then do this trick with your mind.

Tell yourself that for every cup of coffee after 3 cups (let's try to cut it to half), then instead of using your car to go to your grocery shop (a mile away) in the evening you will walk.

Similarly, if you consistently follow any good habit, reward yourself with something, which you like.

As you know, this all is your inside game and no one from the outside is forcing bad habits upon you or stopping you to follow you growth habits. So therefore, you can create such circumstances to help you move towards the desired goal.

Read Literature

"Not all readers are leaders, but all leaders are readers"- Harry S. Truman

Like any other skill in life, you either read the books or you go to some teacher or attend some course, so you should treat the habit development as a skill. It is such an important skill, which if you learn correctly, your whole life will run on auto-pilot.

Imagine a smooth road of clarity in your life moving on a well programmed mindset and powered with rich habits. There won't be any distraction or negative thought affecting you.

I recommend the following people for any new habit formation in your life:

1.   James Clear - http://jamesclear.com/

2.   Leo Babauta - http://zenhabits.net/
3.   Steve Scott - visit
http://www.developgoodhabits.com/

Always Remember your Unshakable Why

And lastly, even at the cost of repetition (because it is of paramount importance) always keep reminding you of your unshakable why and the journey will be always focused and easy. This will keep you motivated and disciplined to form new habits which will lead you towards your end goals.

30 Days Challenge- To Craft Your 30 Hour Day

"Challenges are what make life interesting; overcoming them is what makes life meaningful." -- Joshua J. Marine

Great that you have reached so far and you are now at the last chapter of this Book

If you take this challenge for the next 30 days, then you would be able to quickly see the positive results in your life by implementing the strategies stated in the book. Some benefits may be quite visible in the initial weeks, while you will realize other benefits in the longer period (remember 66 days).

So here is the strategy to best implement the learning in the form of a challenge.

For this challenge, you need to first do some homework. Put your thinking hat on and analyze your last 5 to 10 working days. May be on Saturday morning, with a fresh mind and with your cup of coffee, sitting alone, you need to do the following.

Spare 30 minutes to 1 hour of your free time.

In that one hour, just write it with pen and paper or use your technology and dump all your thoughts about the last week's activities done by you.

Writing something down has a big influence, as it now has come out of your head and you could see it (instead of clutter thoughts in your mind). Now you can take some objective action.

In all these activities, you have to distinguish between two things.

1. What are the activities, which hampered your productivity and curtailed your work pace - term them as "Productivity Killers".
2. What are the activities, which have resulted in improving you speed of work, improved your focus on the important tasks, name them as "Productivity Enhancers".

Examples of the Productivity Killers could be:

1. Having coffee at the coffee dispenser and chatting for 15-30 minutes, skipping your work.
2. Your frequent smoke break (wasting time, money and health).
3. Sitting in a long unproductive meeting.
4. Entertaining an unwanted colleague in your room, stealing your time.
5. Addressing another email popping into your inbox, which increased your emotions of anger or fear and you skipped your work.
6. Keep thinking, your list is yours based on your experience. And write it down.

Examples of Productivity Enhancers could be:

1. Making a priority list in the morning to get the activities done.
2. For all the meeting invites sent to you, asking for a specific agenda and addressing your points, (if you

think they can arise), through email. (Note: this is for routine meetings and not few significant meetings.)

3. Giving you the shorter time to achieve the results.
4. AIC- Putting your Ass in the Chair and keep pushing the work.
5. Re-prioritizing your work every two hours of what to do next, based on the developments of the day.
6. Keeping constant track of your list, how much is done.
7. Drinking and eating healthy beverages or food during your breaks.
8. Drinking lots and lots of water.

Once you have realized that your list reaches to a significant number of activities, then start implementing this two-fold strategy as follows.

1. Everyday choose one Productivity Killer and target it so that it does not hamper you throughout the whole day, whatsoever it may be. Make any excuse, if someone disturbs you etc.
2. Alongside that replace that Productivity Killer with one Productivity Enhancer and focus during the full day to achieve including that in your day schedule.

I know some days would be super unorganized due to various things. So for those days, use the techniques "reduce the scope and stick to the schedule" (remember, you learnt this already).

Follow this one set of two-fold strategy consistently for 3 days.

After that over and above, the first set, add another set of killing one bad habit and enhancing one good habit in your life. Keep adding another set like above after every 3 days.

If you stick to this for 30 days, you will see the domino effect of deleting one bad habit and adding one good habit every week.

Congratulations, you are already on your journey to habit formation. If you stick to the principle taught in this book and implement them, you will see the massive productive results.

Wish you a great success in your productive journey.

Quick Summary to Create Your 30 Hours Day

Congratulations!

After finishing this book, you must have realized by now that unless you make drastic changes in your mindset, belief system and implant new positive habits in your life, achieving productivity would be a distant dream.

But if you implement all such changes in your life, you would not only become super productive; you would be touching the new heights in your career. God Knows, what is awaiting for you, if you keep on delivering in all areas of your life like this.

It might seem some big task at the first sight, but that's how the extra-ordinary lives are made.

"Rome wasn't built in a single day"

"You can't eat the elephant at one go, but it is quite possible, if you do it one bite at a time"

Again it is simple, but not easy.

Below is the summary of what you have learnt and now it is up to you to implement it in your life.

The 30 Hour Day

Productivity Redefined: You need to look at the definition of productivity in a new way. You must understand that the inner game at the macro level is much more important to master before your work on outer material strategies at a micro level.

Mindset: You learnt the different kind of negative mindsets, which hamper your productivity. You further leant that how you can overcome any negative mindset and belief system and replace them with stronger positive and productive mindsets.

Habits: You learnt a ton of positive habits to implement in your life, which will start showing the results immediately in your life. You will start feeling victorious firstly in your inner game, before it appears to the outer world.

Habit formation techniques: You got numerous tricks to form an entirely new set of habits in an easy way. You learnt the significance of discipline in the formation of any habit to be a part of you for the rest of your life.

Challenge: You then took a pledge and made a commitment to accept the challenge to create a productive, stress free life by following the strategies in the book for a period of 30 days. Continuously reminding yourself that you're unshakable "why" is to attain freedom from all stress, attaining the productive life, saving tons of time for the things that matter most to you, this 30 days commitment is really not a big deal.

Finally, thanks a lot for reading and finishing this book.

Even if you could pick up one or two nuggets and improved your life in some manner, that is a great thank you to my work and efforts put in writing this book.

It is also a measure of success for me to write my first book, which was running in my head for quite some time. I also feel this to be an example of productivity in my life, along with my full time job, family with two young kids. So everything is achievable once you develop your inner world to the best of your abilities.

Life is awaiting for a new You.

"Obstacles can't stop you. Problems can't stop you. Most of all, other people can't stop you. Only you can stop you." – J. Gitomer

So work on yourself, be more productive, work smarter, decide faster, earn more and enjoy your life with your loved ones and friends.

****

Thank You!

Before you go, I would like to say thank you for purchasing and reading my book.

You could have picked amongst dozens of other books on this subject, but you took a chance and checked out this one.

So, big thanks for downloading this book and reading all the way to the end.

Now I'd like to ask for a small favor. **Could you please spend a minute or two and leave a review for this book on Amazon at below URL**

http://sombathla.com/the30hourday/review

Reviews are Gold to the Authors!

Your feedback will help me continue to write the kind of Kindle books that help you get results.

And if you loved it, please let me know.

Your Free Gift Bundle:

Did you download your Gift Bundle already?

Click and Download your Free Gift Bundle Below

You can also grab your FREE GIFT BUNDLE through this below URL:

http://sombathla.com/freegiftbundle

ADDITIONAL RESOURCES

Recommended books:

1. **Compound Effect -By Darren Hardy -** To keep you super consistent in actions towards your goals.

2. **Miracle Morning- By Hal Elrod -** The magic tool to start your morning designed, which will help you to unconsciously move faster towards success.

3. **Vision to Reality- By Honoree Corder-** You will learn how the Short term massive actions will turn your life and tons of other techniques and strategies

4. **The One Thing- By Gary Keller-** It will break you tons of myths about the significance of various agendas of your life and finally will help you attain ultimate clarity towards your one thing to focus for a fulfilled life.

5. **The 80/20 Principle: The Secret to Achieving More with Less- By Richard Koch:** This Book will help you to focus on your such activities, which will give you the maximum results for your efforts made.

6. **Eat That Frog: By Brian Tracy:** This is a very short but powerful and action-packed book, which will help you kill your procrastination entirely from the roots. It contains timeless and proven techniques which can be utilized in almost any situations of life and guaranteed to give immense results.

You Tube Videos:

1. The 6 Rituals for ENORMOUS Success! By Robin Sharma. A must watch to rush adrenaline in your body and pumps you up towards fearless action.

https://www.youtube.com/watch?v=xOuYJPdfU2k

Podcast:

You can easily download this podcast on your smartphone or computer by going to iTunes. This is also available for download on android phones.

Achieve you Goals Podcast- Hal Elrod: Weekly podcast by Hal Elrod gives practical tips on different areas of your life from mindsets to skill-sets, with a great dose of motivation towards taking massive action. Here is the link to access the podcast- http://halelrod.com/blog/

About the Author

Som Bathla writes books that focus on changing old mindsets, overcoming self-defeating behavior & best strategies for enhancing the productivity and resourcefulness in all areas of life.

He has written more than half a dozen books and his multiple books have already hit the Amazon #1 Best Seller. He has good plans to continuously create more action guides to help readers to lead a productive and resourceful life (for details visit www.sombathla.com)

He is convinced about the limitlessness of the human potential and strongly believes that everyone has the potential of achieving more than one thinks about oneself. His key life mantra is that a rewarding life is nothing but a series of small actions taken consistently on a daily basis with a positive and resourceful mindset.

Som resides in India where he spends most of his time reading, writing and enjoy with his wonderful family. He is deeply committed to a path of never-ending self-improvement and open to explore the best possibilities coming on his journey.

DISCLAIMER

slight of any individual or organization is purely unintentional.

78392806R00067

Made in the USA
Lexington, KY
09 January 2018